At the start of time it was the Dreaming. This was the beginning of time. In the Dreaming, all the people were animals that lived in other lands. The best way to travel was by water.

One day, some of the animals said that it was time to go. They wanted to live in another country. The animals were looking for better hunting grounds. They went in search of a canoe.

Whale was much bigger than all the other animals. Whale also owned the only canoe big enough to carry them all. Whale was not very friendly and would not lend his canoe to ANYONE.

Starfish was Whale’s only friend. The animals went to Starfish to ask for help to sneak Whale’s canoe away.

One day Starfish said to his friend Whale “You’ve got lots of mullas (head lice)! Let me clean them for you!” Whale agreed and they went to a sunny place on the rocks. Whale could lay in the sun on the rocks. Whale was very happy to get rid of the mullas!

Whale soon fell asleep and was happy and warm on the rocks. The other animals slipped away in the canoe when Starfish gave a signal. Koala, being the strongest, was the main rower. They all rowed the big boat to get away from the land.

Whale woke up and looked to where his canoe was left. It was not there, it was gone! Whale was very angry with his friend Starfish. Whale and Starfish had a big fight. Starfish hit Whale on the top of his head and put a hole in it. Now Whale squirts water out of the top of his head.

Whale was big and strong and Starfish was no match. Whale won the fight when he beat up poor little Starfish. Whale threw him to the bottom of the rock pool. This is where Starfish is today. Starfish still has his scars. Starfish has an old and rough appearance.

Whale then chased the other animals. Whale swam as fast as he could, spurting water out of the hole in his head. They reached land in what is now known as Port Kembla.

Brolga, one of the animals, then stamped a hole in the boat and it sunk. It can be seen at low tide in the harbour. It has now turned to rocks.

Whale is still seen going up and down the coast today. Whale travels to warm waters off New South Wales and Queensland. La Perouse is where Whale looks for his canoe and spurts water from the hole in his head.

Word bank

Dreaming
beginning
travel
canoe
mullas
signal
strongest
squirts
appearance
Brolga
Koala
Kangaroo
Goanna
Port Kembla
harbour
La Perouse